# HELEN SNAPE

D1612778

# Drop the fake smile

## THE RECOVERING PEOPLE-PLEASER'S GUIDE TO SELF-LOVE, BOUNDARIES, AND HEALTHY RELATIONSHIPS

Conscious Dreams
PUBLISHING

Drop the Fake Smile

First Printed in United Kingdom 2023

Published by Conscious Dreams Publishing
www.consciousdreamspublishing.com

Edited by Elise Abram and Daniella Blechner

Cover Design by Emily's World of Design
www.emilysworldofdesign.com

Typeset by Oksana Kosovan

ISBN: 978-1-915522-39-9

# DEDICATION

This book is dedicated to all of us breaking free of people-pleasing and discovering how to enjoy life, relationships and being ourselves.

I want to thank those who made this book possible, including Neil, Caterina, Hannah, FloJo, Danni, and my readers who inspired me.

# THIS BOOK IS FOR YOU IF:

- You want to lead a life you love, without needing the approval of others
- You value connection and harmony and want more rewarding relationships
- You know it is time for you to start speaking up for yourself without feeling guilty or fearing the response

But…

- Right now you feel overwhelmed, taken advantage of, not good enough and resentful. You are fed up of agreeing to things and regretting it, of trying to keep the peace and trying to make everyone happy and of unfulfilling relationships.

When you need a reminder to honour your peace, remember your power and to use your voice, dip into *Drop the Fake Smile*, for encouragement and inspiration. I believe in you.

# CONTENTS

**LOVING BOUNDARIES**

**EFFECTIVE COMMUNICATION**

**FUTURE YOU**

# INTRODUCTION

## Why I wrote this book

Are you familiar with that helpless feeling you have when you've said 'yes' to another person or another task, and you don't know why you've said it? Maybe you find it impossible to make decisions and perhaps you feel that no matter how hard you try, however much you give, you still feel as if you don't get enough back.

I know what it's like. I know how awful it feels, how empty. And how it seems like there is no escape. I have written this book because it is the guidance I needed but couldn't find. I have been figuring out what has worked for me, for my clients, and for those who are on a similar journey, so I can distil that knowledge and experience for you and guide you along your journey, too. I do not hold myself as an expert, but I can tell you what works, and it isn't complicated. Let me be your guiding hand for the journey on which you pick up what resonates with you and leave the rest behind.

I believe we all deserve to live a life we love, and we can only really do that when we have healthy relationships with ourselves, with other people, and with a higher power. When we are stuck in a state of 'disease to please', we behave in ways that ensure we don't get what we so desperately want: connection, attention, and love. The good news is that we can learn how to have healthy relationships even if we didn't experience them in our own families and even if we have experienced unhealthy relationships as adults. I have had to un-learn so much I thought I knew about relationships and start again, and you can do the same, starting right now.

This level of change in your life doesn't happen overnight; it is a journey, and it is totally achievable. I have gone on that journey and seen many others do so, too. You, too, can have confidence, great relationships, peace in your heart, and the ability to create a life you will love.

## A little bit about me

I was the ultimate people-pleaser. I grew up being the 'good girl' — I did as I was told, I got good grades in school, and I loved making other people happy. When I was very young, I wrote stories, sang, and drew for my parents.

At school, I was badly bullied. I am blind in one eye, and that drew the attention of some girls who were on a power trip. No matter what I did or who I told, the bullying continued. I learnt

I was helpless and that it was best to be as invisible as possible. The bullying made it hard for me to have time with friends, and I was so desperate to be with them that any chance I got, I would agree to do whatever they were doing.

I learnt to be a chameleon, fitting in with whoever I was with. If I could make the other person happy, they might spend time with me and like me.

However, when it came to boys, I was a rebel. I always seemed to pick boys my parents thoroughly disapproved of. I married straight after university to the first man who gave me the attention I craved. It was a bad choice, but I didn't know any better. He wanted my life to revolve around his needs and wants and got cross when it didn't. I thought I was being so unselfish, putting him first, but no matter how hard I tried, it was never good enough for him, so I tried harder and harder. I was miserable and empty, but I ignored that.

The turning point came when my mother was diagnosed with myeloma, an incurable cancer that attacks the bone marrow throughout the body. I realised how short life was, how precious it was, and finally, a quiet voice inside of me said, 'Enough is enough. You deserve better.'

And so began my journey of coming back to myself.

The hardest thing I have ever done in my life was to leave my marriage. I had taken my vows seriously, and I was terrified of leaving, of facing life alone, but I knew the choice was to stay and have a complete breakdown or leave and give us both a chance to start over with our separate lives.

I have been on a journey of transformation ever since; through therapy, coaching, bodywork, meditation, reading, and hours and hours of self-reflection and journaling, I know what works, and I support my clients on their own journeys of transformation.

I have learnt the keys you need to go on this journey:

- self-discovery,
- mind-body connection,
- inner child healing,
- loving boundaries, and
- effective communication.

These are the keys to taking that fake smile we wear when we are people-pleasing and turning it into a genuine smile, and I am going to unpack each of them for you.

This book will show you how you, too, can let go of your ineffective people-pleasing patterns of behaviour. You, too, can build a better life for yourself and be fully and bravely yourself without apology.

## What will you get from reading this book?

You will gain an understanding of where your people-pleasing behaviours might have come from, what purpose they serve, and how they show up in your relationships at home, at work, and beyond. You will be given the tools to transform yourself so that you will no longer be held back by not being able to say 'No.' Instead, you will be on a path to create a life that you'll love, knowing that you are and always have been good enough.

You will learn how self-discovery, re-establishing a mind-body connection and a relationship with your Inner Child; building loving boundaries and effective communication are the keys to making this transformation happen.

You deserve a life you love and relationships that are not based on the need to be needed, and instead, are loving and expansive. It starts with the relationship you have with yourself, and you will learn how to have that relationship and actually enjoy time with yourself!

By reading this book, engaging with the exercises offered, reflecting on your own experiences, and trying out some new ideas, you will blossom, and you will be done with your fake smiling.

# PAST YOU

# CHAPTER 1

# What's the Problem with you Being the 'Good Girl'?

For a long, long time, I thought I was doing all the right things. I knew it was good to put others first, to not be greedy, to not make a fuss, to do as I was told, and to be kind and patient with people, so that's what I did. I couldn't understand why I often felt so miserable and empty inside. I tried harder and harder, yet the emptiness seemed to yawn ever wider.

What does people-pleasing actually look like, aside from the more obvious examples, like finding it so hard to say 'No' to people? And what are the consequences for us and other people, in the short-term and in the longer term?

## You can't say 'No' to people

Another way of putting it is that you become an automatic 'Yes' dispenser. Your colleague wants some help with her project. She knows it's not your job to help her, and you know that, too. You also have commitments and deadlines, but she asks you, and you, of course, say, 'Yes, sure, I'd love to help!' Or your friend wants a babysitter for tomorrow evening. You know you have a full day, and you have to get up super-early the following morning for an important meeting, but somehow, a 'Yes, I'll do it!' slips out of your mouth.

In the short term, you will feel tired from over-committing yourself and miserable that you have violated your own boundaries by agreeing to do stuff you don't want to do! This can lead to a cycle of negative thinking because, yet again, you have given in.

In the longer term, you will store up resentment. Even though you said, 'Yes,' you feel cross the person asked you; you feel as if they expected it from you, and that isn't fair. You've sent out a message to both yourself and the world that you come second, and everyone else comes first. You've also sent out the message that there is no cost to them or you when they ask for your help. This, of course, encourages them to come back again and again.

## You get taken advantage of

At least, that's how it feels. For example, you may find that when your sister rings, it's always the same: she spends an hour moaning about her life whilst you listen and make sympathetic noises, and then she has no time left to listen to you. Or it may be that friend who frequently asks you to do favours but never seems able to return those favours to you.

At work, you find that you are the one organising the Christmas dinner, even though you hate organising events, because no one else volunteered, and you are sure it won't happen if you don't step up.

In the short term, you are likely to feel angry or frustrated with other people for overstepping your boundaries, but you also feel angry and frustrated towards yourself because you let them do it. You may also feel inauthentic, as if you are wearing a fake smile because you are not being true to yourself. You are also not being loving to yourself or your Inner Child, who we will get to know later.

In the long term, your resentment builds. You have set others' expectations about you, and that is hard to shift. Being the person everyone dumps on or relies upon is likely to mean you get really busy with endless doing, and the danger is that you will run out of steam, you will fall ill, be exhausted, and ultimately, burn out.

## You avoid conflict and confrontation

You likely take the turtle approach to manage conflict: you hide your head and hope it goes away! When you grow up in an environment where you don't see how to handle conflicts and arguments successfully, you may be terrified of facing them. You are likely to develop strategies to avoid conflict, such as being too busy — 'I've got to run the kids to school, then I must go shopping, then I must do the washing… can't we talk about this later?' — and later never happens. Or you use distractions — 'Oh, yes, we need to talk about that, but did you hear what just happened in the news?' Or you pretend to be ill — 'You know my stomach has been troubling me; why would you bring that up now?'

Sadly, this approach is lose-lose: It neither solves the problem nor nurtures your relationship. You don't address your own needs and wants either.

In the long-term, it damages the relationship, as there will be a lack of honesty, open communication, and intimacy, which contributes to your hiding the real you and feeling alone. It makes you hypervigilant about others' feelings, so you will be ready to deal with them at the first sign of disagreement. You are so tuned into other people's feelings you don't tune into your own through a mind-body connection. It also means you don't get the best that life has to offer. You settle for unsatisfactory situations, events, and relationships because you can't deal with the difficult feelings that come with any sort of conflict.

## You are always putting others' needs before your own

You have taken on board the message that it isn't good to be needy, and you are very careful to put others' needs — and even others' wants — first before your own. For example, maybe you've never chosen which restaurant to eat out at when you meet your friend. Even if your friend were to ask, you would say, 'I don't mind — you choose.' You let others choose what to watch on TV. You help organise the community fair because you know they need your help even though you are already overextended and could use some more rest time.

In the short term, you gain some temporary approval from other people, which can feel good for a little while. However, you are also squishing down your own feelings and ignoring your own needs and wants, and you are not looking after yourself or your Inner Child.

Those feelings don't, however, go away. Remember that mind-body connection? Feelings build up in our bodies if we don't acknowledge and process them at the time they appear or soon after. This is why I have met so many people who are stuck in a people-pleasing pattern for much of their lives and who have developed chronic illnesses — such as IBS, back problems, cancer, fibromyalgia — and/or struggle with depression or anxiety.

Longer-term, it can also damage the very relationships we value so highly because the other person may find it hard to get to know someone who never says what they want or need, which removes the balance of give and take in a relationship.

## Ultimately, where does all this stem from?

As humans, we are social creatures. Evolutionarily speaking, it made sense for us to be part of a tribe, and pleasing others was a good way to avoid being exiled. However, some of us learnt to put that skill into overdrive when our parents weren't well-attuned to our needs or if they met them inconsistently.

I believe we each have a unique earthly experience that shapes how we show up in the world. Although I sometimes talk about 'people-pleasers', I don't believe that is who you are.

People-pleasing is a survival strategy, a pattern, so well ingrained that most of us don't know we are doing it. This pattern consists of thoughts, feelings, behaviours, sensations, and how we use our energies. Think about your own childhood — did you feel seen as a child? Did you feel heard? Did you feel that you could just be yourself? Or were you told you were 'too sensitive' or 'too emotional', and you learnt it wasn't okay to express your feelings? Maybe your parents had difficulty owning and processing their own feelings or getting their own needs met, and they couldn't be there for you to rely on them. When that happens, you develop a brilliant ability, a go-to tactic, to track their moods and do whatever it takes not to rock the boat. Maybe you develop that fake smile.

When one of your parents felt a negative emotion, or they criticised or ignored you, rather than knowing it was about their lives, you felt as if it was your fault and the shame that produced led you to develop the go-to tactic of hiding away and being 'good' or performing to gain attention.

Quite often, there is a pattern of not having your needs — particularly your emotional needs — consistently met or in the way you needed as a child, so you suppress those needs and project your needs out onto other people as an adult. Your go-to tactic is to become the one who takes care of other people's needs. You can also develop the people-pleasing pattern from trying to fit in, where what makes you unique isn't easily accepted. Or as a protective response to trauma.

What is your go-to tactic? Whatever it is, it totally makes sense. Isn't it brilliant that our whole mind-body system creates these patterns to keep us safe?

When we begin to recognise our patterns and own them, we can start to look at alternative ways to keep ourselves safe, and that may be more fruitful for us as adults.

Associated with the pattern of people-pleasing is the feeling of not being enough or not being good enough, so we throw ourselves into over-working because then, maybe, we will be 'good enough'. Or we make ourselves invisible and keep quiet because we feel as if we are not enough, and we seek others' approval because that will surely confirm we are good enough.

It actually leaves us feeling scared of what others might think and having to perform to imagined standards of what we think others expect from us (whether they do or not). We fear for our futures because we feel inadequate. We have low levels of energy because we busy ourselves and distract ourselves from addressing that which we actually need to address. We feel ashamed that we aren't good enough, we feel like fakes, and we do all that fake smiling.

What if all of this is an illusion? What if we *are* good enough? What if our true nature is simply hidden from us, covered over in programming and messages from our childhood patterning, from our family, or from society that we internalised and believe to be true?

How can we break free from years of thinking, feeling, and behaving in ways that perpetuate this cycle to discover the truth of who we really are?

That is what the rest of this book is about. This is where knowing who you truly are, your True Self, will unleash the YOU that lies beneath those people-pleasing patterns. This is where re-establishing that mind-body connection will restore your power on an ongoing basis. This is where learning to truly love yourself and your Inner Child breaks the desire to be needed in relationships, freeing you to create real intimacy and connections with others. This is where building healthy boundaries allows you to stand up for yourself without pushing others away. This is where effective communication enables you to express your feelings, needs, wants, and boundaries in ways that others will understand.

## Exercise 1 — Recognising the signs and raising self-awareness

1. For many of the exercises in this book, including this one, you will be invited to write something. So, first of all, find a pen and some paper. You can download this exercise and all the exercises in this book from my website.

   www.helensnape.com/dropthefakesmile

   I prefer a pen and paper over typing my answers and ideas on a device, but do what works for you.

2. Set aside 20 minutes for this exercise. Find somewhere where you can be alone and undisturbed.

3. Below are 12 signs you are people-pleasing. Tick the ones that apply to you. Even if you don't do it all the time, ask yourself if it's true for you most of the time. This is an exercise to raise awareness, *not* to judge yourself. We can only start to change that of which we are aware.

   ☐ You can't say no to people.

   ☐ You get taken advantage of.

   ☐ You avoid conflict and confrontation.

   ☐ You put others' needs before your own.

   ☐ You feel responsible for other people's feelings.

   ☐ You pretend everything is fine when it isn't.

☐ You adapt to fit in with whoever you are with.

☐ You do things out of a sense of obligation.

☐ You struggle to make decisions on your own.

☐ You make compromises and promises you later regret.

☐ You feel the need to be needed in relationships.

☐ You say what you think will change the other person's behaviour.

4. Write about the impact being stuck in people-pleasing patterns has had on each of these areas of your life: health, wealth, career, intimate relationships, family, friends, and spirituality.

_____

_____

_____

_____

_____

_____

_____

_____

5. Spend some time thinking about where these patterns might have developed in your life and write down what comes up for you.

_____

_____

_____

_____

_____

_____

_____

_____

# SELF-DISCOVERY

# CHAPTER 2

# You Are Not Your Thoughts

I was panting from being out of breath after running back to the shop for more milk. My husband had already berated me for not having all the ingredients to make dinner and because I was in danger of serving it up late, I felt so guilty. I had agreed that I had been careless, and I hurried to the local shop to pick up more vegetables, but I had forgotten the milk.

My head was so jumbled from all the shouting that I couldn't remember even the short shopping list. As I ran back to the shop for the second time, I told myself that I was so stupid. How could I forget the milk? Had I done it deliberately because he'd shouted at me? That showed how mean and selfish I must have really been. Now I was going to be late making dinner, and I knew how important it was that he ate on time! I kept trying, and I kept failing.

I believed it all. My thoughts were my thoughts, after all, so if I told myself these things, I must believe them and be the terrible person my thoughts told me I was. I knew, from reading some Christian pamphlets when I was at university, that I couldn't trust my emotions. Emotions were fleeting things, and I felt so utterly miserable so much of the time that I would rather ignore them, anyway.

That was how unconscious I was. It is also how many, many people live their lives. You identify with your thoughts and believe that whatever you think about yourself must be true.

But it's a lie.

**We are not our thoughts.**

The beginning of my awakening was the occasional shift of my awareness from being in my head, wrapped up in my thoughts and feelings, to what felt like an observer's seat up high, looking down on my life. I remember it happening at a party my husband and I went to. There were all these clever, interesting people there. My husband expected me to stay by his side and only leave in order to fetch him food or drink. I really wanted to talk with some of the other people and enjoy their company, even if it was only for a couple of hours. This awareness from my newly found 'Observer seat' helped me see the bigger picture of the party and how silly it was for a fully capable man to expect me to trail after him all evening.

Even though I'd enjoyed the evening, I left early. When my husband came home many hours later, he was furious with me. He'd apparently flown into a rage with several people at the party, and he blamed me for not keeping him adequately hydrated and fed and for leaving early. The enjoyment of the party fell away, replaced by leaden guilt. Scared, I apologised, but it didn't help. He still seethed. My 'Observer awareness' kicked in again. It felt as if I was looking at both of us from high above, and I could see how ridiculous his accusations were. I could see how we fitted together like two jigsaw pieces, him being angry and demanding and me being soft and yielding. It wasn't right, my Observer awareness told me.

Now I know that the awareness within me was my True Self, the part of me that knew the truth and knew what was best for me. It was that part of me that got me to ask for help and find a therapist, but it only appeared some of the time. It wasn't until I learnt about meditation and mindfulness that my inner world opened up to me.

These concepts and practices will be key for you, too, both for discovering yourself and re-establishing your mind-body connection.

## Turn your attention inwards

If you, like me, are used to spending much of your time thinking about other people — what they are thinking, what they are feeling, what they need, and what they might do next — it's time to turn that beautiful attention you give to everyone else onto yourself. When something happens, begin to ask yourself, 'What do *I* think?' 'What do *I* feel?'

The reason why this is so important is that **the first step to any kind of change is awareness**. If you never focus on what you think or feel, your life is unlikely to change. Behaviour transforms as a result of changes to your thoughts and feelings.

## The observer seat

Imagine that you are sitting on a cloud, looking down at yourself and your life and that you know everything there is to know about you.

• What do you notice that you didn't before?

_____

_____

_____

_____

- What do you notice about how you are living your life?

_____

_____

_____

_____

- What patterns are showing up in your relationships?

_____

_____

_____

_____

- What recurring thoughts do you have every day?

_____

_____

_____

_____

- Which feelings do you let yourself feel?

_____

_____

_____

_____

- Which ones do you stop yourself from feeling?

_____

_____

_____

_____

Take five minutes every day to stop, find a quiet place, and sit in silence. Either close your eyes or soften your gaze and notice which thoughts and feelings arise. When they appear, let them appear. Let them disappear, too; don't hold onto them.

This very simple practice will unlock so much of the change you are going to make.

## Finding your own thoughts and feelings

Even if, at this stage, you are not sure what you do think or feel, just keep asking the questions and notice what comes up for you in your mind and in your body.

See what sensations arise. For example, you might notice that your chest feels tighter, you have tensed your shoulders, or your stomach feels hot. Great! You are learning your body's cues to emotions. You are strengthening your mind-body connection, which we will explore in more detail in Section 3.

You can make this into a daily practice in the morning and at night.

You might find it useful to write your observations down. Even if you don't feel confident writing or you think you won't enjoy it, get yourself a journal or a notebook and give it a go. When we get our thoughts and feelings onto paper, it helps us see what we really do think and feel, which brings us greater clarity.

Now, the crucial thing to remember when you turn your attention inwards, notice any judgement you have of your thoughts and feelings and let them go. Imagine these judgments are clouds floating across the sky — they appear, and then they disappear from view.

For example, you might think, 'I don't want to talk to that person; they tire me out,' and you immediately think, 'Oh, wow. I am being really selfish, and it's surely not that person's fault that I feel tired when I talk with them. There must be something wrong with me.' And on it goes!

Remember that the thought and the follow-on thoughts are NOT YOU. You can notice them with interest, but you don't have to believe them.

### Reacting vs responding

You might also notice when you react to situations as if you were on 'autopilot'.

For example, when a friend invites you out for dinner and asks you where you would like to go, your automatic reaction might be to ask them back, 'Where would *you* like to go?' This is because you have grown up putting everyone else's needs and wants before your own, so this feels like familiar territory to you.

Our automatic reactions are our brains taking the well-known route. We have spent years developing a belief system and knowledge of how the world works, so when something happens, it's easiest for our brain to do what it has always done, but that doesn't mean it's still what is best for us.

Becoming aware of our automatic reactions invites the possibility of changing them. At first, you are likely to only notice them some of the time, most likely well after they have occurred, and that's fine. You can begin to explore what might be other ways of responding, so you will consciously respond in a way that serves you best.

Gradually, you will begin to notice your reactions in real-time and have more choice as to whether to let them unfold or stop them and choose a different way of interacting.

## Exercise 2 — Your thoughts and feelings

This is an exercise to do every day over the next week (and beyond!) to take you on a journey of self-discovery, and it will only take you five minutes. Remember, you can download this exercise and all the exercises in this book from my website.

www.helensnape.com/dropthefakesmile

1. Give yourself five minutes, and if possible, grab your pen and paper to record your reflections.

2. Breathe slowly in and out a couple of times, and then use these two journaling prompts:

   • 'Today I feel...'
   • 'Right now, I need...'

   Write down whatever comes up for you. Remember that there are no rights or wrongs here.

_____

_____

_____

_____

_____

_____

3. Practise, through journaling or meditation, observing your thoughts and feelings each day. Use these prompts to help you:

- What recurring thoughts do I have?
- What feelings keep coming up?
- Which feelings do I push away?
- Do these thoughts and feelings come up with particular people?

# CHAPTER 3

# Who You Are When No-one is Watching

As a small child, I loved to sing and dance, preferably both at the same time, to ABBA music. I could express how I was feeling through the music in a way I felt I couldn't verbalise. Dancing and singing, especially if no one was watching, was a way for me to be free and in the moment.

When I got married, the music stopped.

Occasionally, I would listen to music with my husband, and I enjoyed those times very much, but at other times, music annoyed him, and annoying him would invite his anger. Also, I walked on eggshells, feeling as if I had to be attentive to whatever he needed. He expected me to hear him wherever he was and give him my full attention, so it wouldn't do to be playing music. I think it also annoyed him if I was having 'too much' fun.

I didn't realise how squashed I felt as a person back then.

When I left, one of the first things I did was play music loudly and dance around my flat. I have since tried all different kinds of dancing, from Bollywood to Bachata, but so far, my favourite form of dance is free-form, madly waving my arms and legs about as the music moves me. I feel so happy and alive doing that. What I later came to learn was how dancing aligned with some of my top core values of fun, learning, love, and safety, and it all made total sense.

## Find your joy

Think back to when you were a child — what did you love to do? What made you smile? How would you spend your time when you had the choice? Does any of what you loved then show up in your life today? If not, what would it be like to re-introduce an element of it?

Giving yourself experiences that bring you joy or doing something just for fun is an expression of loving yourself and your Inner Child that is easy to accomplish, so go do it!

### Who are you when no one is watching?

Are you the same person as you are when interacting with your spouse? Your children? Your parents? Your colleagues? Your friends?

I trained in personality profiling during my career in human resources, and each individual had two resulting profiles: how you show up when you know you are being watched and how you show up when you think you aren't. For some people, it's the same or very close, and for others, they are quite different. There are no rights and wrongs here, but it does is raise a few questions.

What might be the reason for this shift? Is it a conscious choice? Do you adapt yourself to 'fit in' with those around you? Do you mould yourself to others' expectations of how you *should* show up as a mother, a CEO, a daughter, and so on? What energy does it cost to keep adapting? Is it worth it?

### What is important to you

When I started my training in transformational coaching, one of the early lessons was about identifying your core values. This is simply what is important to you, what motivates you, and what gets you out of bed in the morning. It is also informed by what really irritates you.

They are important because when you live in alignment with your core values, you feel more at peace. They help you to know yourself, identify what is okay for you and what isn't, and become the basis for building your loving boundaries.

When you feel stuck, sometimes it arises from a conflict between two of your values, and so understanding what they are becomes even more important. I have had times in my venture to speak in public when I have felt stuck because, whilst I loved the learning and feedback process, I didn't feel safe, and therefore, it wasn't fun. While the opportunity to learn was there, and learning is one of my top values, the fun and safety values weren't being met. I needed to find environments where I felt held, and then I blossomed.

When somebody upsets or annoys you, you may discover that it goes against your values in some way. I would get annoyed with students who deliberately disrupted the class in school and college because I felt it disrespected my value of learning.

You can begin to figure out your values by brainstorming them. At the end of the chapter is a list of values to help you, but don't feel restricted by them. There are no rights and wrongs here, and everyone's values will be different.

Seeking out what brings you joy, knowing and honouring your values, and living your life as if no one is watching is all about you embracing *you*, your true self, showing yourself that *you* matter and taking your needs seriously.

## Exercise 3 — What matters to you is important!

Set aside 20 minutes for this exercise and have your pen and paper in hand. To make it easier, you can download this exercise and all the exercises in this book from my website.

www.helensnape.com/dropthefakesmile

1. Start off by brainstorming what your values are. There are no right or wrong answers here. If you want some extra inspiration, below is a list of values to give you more ideas. You can tick which ones matter to you. What you are doing here is capturing what's important to you and what motivates you. This is going to be entirely unique to you.

☐ Humour                ☐ Contribution
☐ Participation          ☐ Community
☐ Freedom of choice      ☐ Performance
☐ Connection             ☐ Excellence
☐ Co-operation           ☐ Focus
☐ Playfulness            ☐ Empathy
☐ Power                  ☐ Productivity
☐ Honesty                ☐ Support
☐ Acknowledgement        ☐ Romance
☐ Lightness              ☐ Family
☐ Recognition            ☐ Spirituality
☐ Harmony                ☐ Empowerment

| | | | |
|---|---|---|---|
| ☐ | Accomplishment | ☐ | Self-expression |
| ☐ | Orderliness | ☐ | Integrity |
| ☐ | Creativity | ☐ | Independence |
| ☐ | Accuracy | ☐ | Nurturing |
| ☐ | Joy | ☐ | Adventure |
| ☐ | Beauty | ☐ | Authenticity |
| ☐ | Spontaneity | ☐ | Freedom |
| ☐ | Dependability | ☐ | Serenity |
| ☐ | Respect | ☐ | Elegance |
| ☐ | Growth | ☐ | Vitality |
| ☐ | Aesthetics | ☐ | Success |
| ☐ | Trust | ☐ | Uniqueness |
| ☐ | Love | ☐ | Fairness |
| ☐ | Being active | ☐ | Ambition |
| ☐ | Safety | ☐ | Security |
| ☐ | Excitement | ☐ | Change |
| ☐ | Curiosity | ☐ | Bravery |
| ☐ | Personal growth | ☐ | Kindness |

2. You may have a short or long list of values you have identified as being important to you. Either way is perfect.

3. If you have more than ten values on your list, have a go at highlighting your top ten values (go with your gut instinct

here, and don't forget to group similar or connected things together under one word).

4.  See if you can narrow your list down to your top five values.

5.  For your top five values, write out what each of them means to you in the different areas of your life, for example:

    - your work,
    - your family,
    - your health,
    - your well-being, and so on.

_____

_____

_____

_____

_____

_____

_____

_____

_____

_____

_____

_____

_____

_____

_____

_____

_____

6. Find a way to remind yourself of your values on a regular basis. You might want to create a visual reminder or create a reminder on your phone.

# MIND-BODY CONNECTION

# CHAPTER 4

# Your Feelings Matter

I often ask clients how they feel about a situation in their lives. Often, the reply is 'I don't know,' quickly followed by a detailed description of how their partner, mother, friends, and so on feel about it. When we have spent our lives tuning into how other people feel, we are often out of touch with how *we* feel and don't stop to consider that it matters.

I have often been told that I am empathetic and sensitive to others' feelings. This is ironic because, until relatively recently, I found connecting with my 'big' emotions a difficult and sometimes frightening process.

## Why your feelings matter

I remember, as a teenager, being bullied at secondary school because I had acne. I hated how I looked, and my poor skin often felt sore, itchy, and either very dry or oily. My parents did their best to help me feel better, telling me to ignore the other children and that I was really pretty. Mum would help me find increasingly potent treatments for my skin with increasingly severe side effects. Eventually, I had a private consultation with a dermatologist who suggested we try the nuclear option: a six-month programme of antibiotics. My poor body. Still, it did clear my acne in that period and for another six months after. Then it all came back.

When I came home miserable from both the soreness of my face and being bullied about it, I needed validation of my experience and how I felt, and not told to 'just ignore them', thereby ignoring my reality. I needed a loving container for my sadness and by that point, well-buried anger. I didn't feel I had that in the way I needed, so I tucked the emotions away and grew a big pool of sadness and anger inside.

I read recently how a study with teenagers with acne[1] showed that giving them self-compassion exercises to do proved effective in reducing both the feelings of depression and shame around acne. It had also proven effective when it came to how bothered they felt

1   Kelly, A.C., Zuroff, D.C., & Shapira, L.B. (2009). The healing power of self-kindness. Soothing Oneself and Resisting Self-Attacks: The Treatment of Two Intrapersonal Deficits in Depression Vulnerability. *Cognitive Therapy Research 33*, 301–313.

physically, with a reduction in burning and stinging sensations. Isn't that fascinating? It also points to what was missing for me.

On my recovery journey, I have learnt how to give myself the kind of loving, understanding, and empathy I needed, as well as form healthier relationships in which my feelings would be honoured.

You can do this, too.

## What are feelings?

I like to describe feelings as having three parts: Emotion, Movement, and Energy.

### Emotion

This is the label you give to how you are feeling, such as angry, sad, delighted, scared, guilty, and so on. There is something powerful about being able to name our experiences. However, don't get hung up on labels. If you can't find suitable words to capture your feelings, it doesn't matter. What's important is *experiencing* them.

### Movement

When someone asks you how you feel, how do you know? We sometimes think it's coming from our brain when actually, it's coming from our whole bodies, including our brains. There is a movement within which we often don't notice that tells us what we are feeling. The movement may be a change in sensation from hot to cold, from dry to damp, from stillness to activity, or from openness to tightness. When I feel grief, for example, I feel a tight gripping of my heart, and my upper body wants to curl inwards. When I feel love, I feel expansive and relaxed.

## Energy

Everything is energy, including our bodies and emotions. Some emotions carry lower vibration energies, such as shame, guilt or anger, and that's often why we feel 'heavy' with them. Others are a higher vibration, such as love and joy.

You can now see how emotions are dynamic and need to flow through us. When we ignore, deny, or minimise how we feel, they can get 'stuck' and build up in our bodies, leading to longer-term problems. As we re-establish our mind-body connections, we can let those feelings flow through us like waves in the ocean.

## Letting your feelings inform you

Somewhere along the way, I picked up the erroneous message that feelings were not to be trusted, that they would throw you off course and hinder you from reaching your goals. This was reinforced when I got 'too' emotional to think straight and couldn't move forward.

But it wasn't true.

What is true is that our feelings have really useful information for us, and we ignore them at our peril. There is a balance to be had. I often use the analogy of a car. We don't want our emotions to drive the car, so they can erupt all over other people when we say things we regret and unnecessarily damage relationships. Neither do we want to lock our emotions in the boot of the car, ignoring the essential information they might give us about the person we are with, the environment, and the situation.

Our feelings are important passengers in the car. We want to listen to them by allowing that mind-body connection, tuning into them, and doing two things: firstly, asking ourselves whether our feelings reflect our current circumstances, and secondly, letting our feelings inform our actions.

The first question helps us determine whether our feelings have arisen in response to something that is actually happening *now*, in the present moment, or as a response to something similar that happened in the past (of which we are not consciously aware). It is not about whether our feelings are 'right' or 'wrong' because there are no right or wrong feelings. A good question to ask yourself is whether your feelings seem 'over the top', or not needed for the current situation. This may be an indication that a past trigger has come up for you. If you have been triggered, make a note of it and come back to work through it at a later time. Then, let your feelings inform your actions.

You might decide to feel the feeling and let it go, or you might decide to funnel the energy of that emotion into your actions. For example, if you feel angry because someone is interrupting you, that anger fuels you to protect your boundary, either by naming the interruption and asking them not to do it or by choosing to no longer continue the conversation.

## Tuning into your feelings

How do you really know what you are feeling?

Firstly, *slow down*. We live in a society of instant gratification and feedback. We can ask ourselves how we are feeling and only listen to what our minds immediately answer. Our minds aren't necessarily right. Our bodies go at a slower pace.

When you ask yourself, 'How am I feeling?' turn your attention in towards your core. Your core is the middle of you. Imagine a line from the top of your head down through your heart and stomach, all the way down to your pelvis, and *wait* for the answer to come.

You may notice that your attention is drawn to a particular place in your body. You might notice a sensation such as warmth or buzzing, movement, or knowing.

You might then notice if there is anything else to describe, such as a texture, a colour, or a shape. You might notice if there are words or a message or a voice.

If you try this way of feeling your feelings and find it hard to feel anything, give yourself patience and kindness. You *DO* have feelings; we all do. Sometimes, it takes a while to feel them when we have spent so long, and we get so good at denying them, ignoring them, and minimising them.

## Exercise 4 — Tuning into your feelings

It is common for us to go through the day not really aware of our emotions or how we are feeling. This is a meditation to help you tune into your feelings. You can download the mp3 audio of this meditation at www.helensnape.com/dropthefakesmile, or you can follow the text version here:

We are going to take this time for you to connect gently with your emotions without being overwhelmed. Remember that there are no 'bad' emotions. All emotions are welcome here. When we are able to feel our feelings, we allow them to pass through.

Find a comfortable position, either sitting upright or lying down. Relax. Get comfortable. Gently close your eyes or soften your gaze.

Notice your breathing. There is no need to change how you are breathing; just notice its rhythm in and out. Notice how the breath comes in through your nose and fills up your belly. Notice how it travels back up the spine and out again.

Thank yourself for giving yourself this time to connect with your emotions. Say 'thank you' either in your mind or out loud three times.

Thank you.

Thank you.

Thank you.

What do you notice in your body when you say thank you? Perhaps you feel a warmth in your chest, a lump in your belly, or a tightness of your throat.

Thank you.

Now ask yourself: 'How am I feeling? How am I *really* feeling?'

Notice where you seek to find the answer. It may be that, at first, you look to your mind. See if you can bring your attention below your chin as it is in the body that you will find the real answers.

Notice where your attention goes in your body when you ask, 'How am I feeling?'

What sensation do you feel there? Is there a shape there? Is there a colour? A texture?

If that sensation could speak to you, what would it say?

Take your time to absorb all of the messages from your body. If you notice your mind wandering, know that this is normal. Just gently return your attention to your body.

Now, place a hand on that part of your body — what do you notice when you place your hand there?

What messages does your body have for you?

Ask yourself what you need at this moment. Maybe it's rest, tenderness, or connection.

Thank yourself again for taking this time to connect with your emotions.

Thank you.

Let your hands come to your heart, and let yourself absorb all the feelings and possibilities of this meditation.

Now, come back to focus on your breath. Breathe in the light of the universe.

When you are ready, become aware of your fingers and toes. Maybe wiggle them a bit.

And when you are ready, slowly open your eyes and go on to live in your peace and power.

# INNER CHILD

# CHAPTER 5

# Letting Go of the Stories

We all carry stories with us as if we were carrying around heavy rucksacks.

One of my favourite stories was 'No one wants to hear what I have to say'. I was convinced of that. I could point to all the times I would speak up in team meetings at work only to be seemingly ignored. Then, someone else would make the same point five minutes later and get all the credit. I could point to all the conversations I had with friends where they would talk about themselves for hours and not seem bothered that they hadn't learnt anything about my life.

Of course, my ex-husband only wanted to hear praise and gratitude. He did not want to hear about my concerns or worries.

Now I see what a self-fulfilling cycle I had myself in. The more I believed that no one wanted to hear what I had to say, the more I kept quiet and deflected attention away from myself. So, it is perhaps not surprising that people didn't ask my opinion. Even when I did speak up, it wasn't with any confidence or conviction. I surrounded myself with people who loved to talk, share their opinions, and filled in any conversational slack on my part.

I didn't like the state of affairs, but it was familiar, and in some ways, it felt safe; no one was going to yell at me or dislike me if I didn't voice an opinion.

It wasn't until I found a therapist that I truly felt that there was someone who really wanted to hear what I had to say. He really had time for me. I could be open and honest, and he still wanted to hear me talk. Thus began the end of the story I told myself, that no one wanted to listen to me.

Gradually, I opened up and shared my story with friends, then in the supportive environment of my local Toastmasters Club (a public speaking club), then at a networking event, and then at a global summit.

People *did* want to hear what I had to say.

I began to see that I had been telling myself a story; a story that wasn't true.

Huh.

And if *that* story wasn't true, other stories I had been telling myself perhaps weren't true either.

## It's not personal

Sometimes it's about letting go of the meaning we attach to events. We love to ask, 'But what does it mean?' and we have a tendency to make that meaning about ourselves, often in a negative way. For example, if your manager at work says, 'I want to talk to you when you have a minute,' what is your reaction?

For a lot of people, there is an immediate feeling of panic and a desperate internal query of 'What have I done wrong?' followed by an armoury of justifications ready to use as to why they chose to do things one way or another when actually, they didn't know what their manager wanted to talk to them about. It could have been about a promotion opportunity, an IT issue, an office refurbishment, or something else!

A useful exercise in such a situation is to first remember to breathe, and secondly, to ask, 'What do I know is fact and truth here?' You might reason, 'My manager wants to talk with me. Okay. And that's all. There is no further information.' Then, we have a choice: to let our minds wander into all the negative possibilities or let the situation go.

## The messages we grew up with

Sometimes, our stories come from all sorts of messages we receive as we grow up. Even if we consciously reject these messages, some of them sink in on some unconscious level. Do any of these resonate with you?

It's polite to be quiet.
Good girls do as they are told.
Girls should look pretty.
I should be grateful.
I should put others before myself.
I don't have any needs.
I should be able to do it all by myself.
Getting angry is wrong.
I'm not good enough.

These are messages we absorb growing up, but it doesn't mean they are true.

When you notice this sort of message or voice in your head, know that this is your inner critic, a part of your ego. It doesn't know what is true; it just knows what strategies have helped you to survive and to 'fit in' in life so far. That is the job of the ego: to keep you safe and alive!

When viewed this way, you can see that your inner critic is only trying to help you. The problem is that it is stuck in the past and doesn't know there are other options available.

As a part of our journey towards learning to love ourselves, we can begin to befriend that inner critic and learn to tune into the voice of our True Selves.

## Befriending your inner critic

How do you deal with your inner critic? Some people try to ignore it, but that doesn't tend to work very well. Whatever arises from within you, whether they are feelings, thoughts or sensations, they arise for a reason, and they want your attention. If you don't give them any attention, they get louder or find another way to get your attention.

We want to turn our attention towards our inner critics, not to agree with them, but to listen to them and receive their message with thanks. Remember that it is only trying to help!

You can see it like this: you are the CEO of YOU, and within you are all of these different parts. Your ego has many pieces, including the inner critic. There is also your Inner Child, who we will meet properly in the next chapter. Like any good CEO, your job is to look after and listen to *all* of your parts, thank them for their contribution, and then you—your True Self—decide what the way forward is.

## Exercise 5 — Letting go of stories

Time to grab pen and paper again and set aside about 20 minutes. Remember, you can download this exercise and all the exercises in this book from my website.

www.helensnape.com/dropthefakesmile

1. Write down a story or belief your inner critic tells you about yourself that you would like to let go of.

_____

_____

_____

_____

_____

_____

_____

_____

_____

_____

_____

2. Ask your inner critic out loud: 'What is it that you want to tell me?' and wait for a response. You might hear or see words, just have a knowing, see a picture, or a memory might come up. Listen to what your inner critic says.

3. Write what your inner critic says down on your paper. For example, it might be something like, 'I am not good enough,' or 'I shouldn't do that.'

_____

_____

4. Re-write these comments as 'You' statements (e.g., *You* are not good enough; *you* shouldn't do that). Notice what difference this makes for you. This should give you some space and distance from these thoughts.

_____

_____

5. Ask, 'Is this 100% true 100% of the time?' Find one time it hasn't been true, and see if there are other times it hasn't been true. Write it down. By doing this, we bring in our True Selves, who can see that the beliefs don't hold up under scrutiny.

_____

_____

6.  Ask your True Self what you could believe instead that would be more empowering. Wait for an answer and write it down.

_____

_____

7.  Speak your new belief out loud *slowly*. Let it sink in. Speak it out loud again. Speak it whilst looking at yourself in the mirror.

8.  Make this an affirmation you will come back to every day for the next month. Speak it out loud and slowly each time until it sinks in.

# CHAPTER 6

# Falling in Love with Yourself

When I went to university, I found Christianity. I was surrounded by genuinely loving people, fellow students, and people from the church. It was both amazing and overwhelming for me. It brought me face-to-face with a central problem I had been avoiding: whilst I believed those people loved me, and I believed that God loved me, it was too overwhelming to feel their love, and *I* didn't love myself.

If God loved me, I knew I must be lovable, except I just couldn't do it for myself; it was incredibly painful.

I wanted to be a good Christian, and I took up the 'love others as you love yourself' commandment seriously, except that I couldn't do the loving myself part. I figured that if I loved God and He loved me, and I did my part in loving others, eventually, it would all come out right, but it never did.

**When we close our hearts to protect them from further hurt, we also close them off from receiving the love we so desperately need.**

Twenty years later, I had a breakthrough. I discovered that inside of me lived my Inner Child. She was me as a young child, and she was scared and lonely. No one had been looking after her. I could see how precious and beautiful my Inner Child was, and I wanted to give her the love, attention, and protection she so desperately needed. I didn't know how to do that, but I was determined to learn.

Inside of you, too, lives your Inner Child, who you were from about age zero to six. They represent you before you started trying ways to 'fit in' with others, before you started moulding yourself into who you thought your parents needed you to be for them. This is the part of you that holds your creativity, playfulness, spontaneity, passion, and true emotions.

Your Inner Child is young, and they need your love.

Too often, we get caught in a trap, trying to fill this love void with external sources, especially other people, but it is not their job to do this for us. It is too much to require it of others, and they can't do it, besides. *You* are the one your Inner Child has been seeking. Don't palm them off to someone else — it won't work.

### Getting to know your Inner Child

If you have never met your Inner Child before, you can do so in a number of ways. At the end of this chapter are some writing prompts you can use to get started if you like writing. There are meditations, too. You may want the support of a therapist or coach if it feels like too much to do alone.

When you first meet your Inner Child, do so with an open mind and without expectations. You don't know how they are going to react. They may welcome you. They might also ignore you or get angry with you. However they react, it's okay. Your job is to let them know who you are (i.e., that you are the adult version of them, how old you are, what you have achieved, and what year it is now). As an unconscious part of you, they don't know these things! Let them know that you are there for them, that you love them, and that you will find out what they need from you.

Don't worry about what they might ask you — a young child's needs are pretty easy to fulfil. Maybe they will want a hug, reassurance, or to ask you a question. This is only the start of your relationship with your Inner Child. It will develop and grow as long as you commit to spending time with them and honouring their needs.

This is not a sprint. This is something to go slowly with. The goal isn't to move on, it's to bring this part of you into your experience, to honour your childhood and integrate it into your life.

As you develop this relationship with your Inner Child, you will know you have something and someone worth protecting and loving.

## The comparison game

Have you ever had the experience of making something — maybe a recipe, artwork, or a design you were really pleased with — only for the pleasure and sense of accomplishment to disappear when you saw what your friend or colleague had produced? Maybe you look at other families and feel jealous or resentful because they seem to have such a lovely and together family compared to yours. You wonder where you are going wrong, and maybe there is something wrong with you. Yes, it must all be your fault.

Ouch.

The comparison game is painful, isn't it?

Stop comparing yourself to other people. No one in the entire universe is like you. No one else has walked in your shoes and had the same life experiences, the same obstacles, the same family, the same community, and the same struggles.

When we fall into playing the comparison game, our self-worth hinges on how we measure up relative to other people. It's that external focus all over again.

**Beautiful soul, bring your attention back to yourself, your own life. You don't need to prove anything. You are worthy just as you are.**

Whenever you notice yourself comparing yourself to others, congratulate yourself for noticing and choose to stop comparing.

## Self-talk

It is said we have about 90,000 thoughts each day. Most of them are repeated from one day to the next, and the majority of them are negative.

How you talk to yourself matters. We can't control what initial thoughts pop into our minds, but when we become aware of them, we can choose whether to dwell on them or let them go.

When you make a mistake, how do you talk to yourself?

Recently my partner knocked over his cup of coffee, which wasn't remarkable.

Except it totally was.

It was a full cup of hot, black coffee, and it covered the coaster and soaked through the tablecloth and the blanket beneath it.

Rich, hot coffee everywhere.

And my partner's reaction?

'Oh, dear,' he said, in a matter-of-fact kind of way, as if it was no more significant than flipping on a light switch.

Had he not seen the disaster unfolding? Was he not stressed about how to get the coffee out of the fabric?

Nope. None of it.

That was when it struck me what self-compassion looked like.

See, I remember, growing up, that if I knocked over a cup of tea (because I don't drink coffee) all over the dining table, it would be the cue for much drama.

My dad would have said something like, 'Oh, Helen,' in that voice, 'why don't you look where you put things?'

My mum would have been on instant clean-up duty.

My brothers would have laughed and called me names.

And I would have sat there, frozen, not knowing what to do.

I would have felt upset, scared, bad, and ashamed.

I would tell myself off and quiz myself: 'I'm so stupid. How did I let that happen? Now, Mum's all upset. Dad's cross. My brothers are being mean. What's wrong with me?'

I would add it to all the other examples of my not living the perfect life; add it to the growing evidence that there must be something wrong with me.

Well, that was then. I now know that not everything I believe is true! And I know there is nothing wrong with me.

I know the universe was giving me a window into what it is like when your go-to response is self-compassion.

It's beautiful.

Next time I knock over my cup of tea, I am going to tell myself, 'Aww, poor me, I was looking forward to that. I will make myself a new one.'

What's your go-to response?

For most of us, our inner critic pops up with things like, 'You did it again. How stupid are you?' Or 'You don't really care enough to get it right,' or 'You're not as intelligent as you think.'

How about if, when such thoughts come up, you acknowledge the part of you that is scared and then choose to talk to yourself kindly?

What would you say to your best friend if they made the same mistake? You would probably say something like, 'Hey, it's okay. Everyone makes mistakes. You are human, after all.' How would you say it? I'd bet you would say it with kindness and understanding.

What if you become your own best friend? You could then acknowledge your own difficult feelings with gentleness, reflect on how it relates to the wider human experience, and offer yourself some self-compassion.

**Self-care**

Self-care is a practical way to show yourself and your Inner Child love and compassion. First of all, there are the basics: eating, sleeping, movement, connection, intellect, emotion, and spirit.

Are you eating what your body needs? Don't listen to what others say. Trust your body to guide you. You might find yourself craving broccoli, orange juice, or eggs. Give yourself what your body needs for nutrition.

When we don't get enough sleep, it can affect our moods, our concentration, our memory, our relationships, and our resilience.

Do you get enough sleep? When you are tired, do you keep going, or do you have a rest? During the day, do you take regular breaks?

Our bodies are designed for movement. Sedentary work and lives can deplete our energies and lead to health problems. You need to find the movement you enjoy. Don't simply pick running because you think you should do it or because you saw that a friend is training to run a marathon. Find what suits you and your body. Maybe that is walking, dancing, swimming, or yoga.

We are social creatures, and we won't survive without connection. Part of your self-care is to find mutually rewarding connections with other people and with animals. These are connections that make you feel safe and comfortable, where you can be yourself. If you don't have any right now, seek them out. Focus on things you enjoy doing and are interested in, and you will find 'your people'.

We have these amazing minds, and if they aren't given much to do, it can breed overthinking, anxiety, and negative self-talk. Give your mind work to do instead. It may have to do with your work, volunteering, a home project, or getting creative. It's where you direct your brain to invent, categorise, analyse, draw comparisons, draw on memories, make predictions, solve problems, and so on. This way, you can direct your mind down fruitful and positive paths rather than let your mind wander into the 'what's wrong' talk.

Self-care is also about taking care of our emotions, feeling our feelings, and letting them inform our actions. When you notice a difficult feeling arise, what do you do? Do you feel it or repress it? Does it vary with the situation, who you are with, or how tired you are?

How do you nourish your spirit? Does that mean anything to you? We will explore this further in Chapter 10, but for now, have a think about whether your self-care includes your spiritual life.

In addition to these self-care basics, you can adapt your self-care to what you need on different days. The simple way to do this is to check in regularly with yourself, particularly at the beginning of each day, and ask, 'What do I need right now?'

This is so simple, yet it will have an extraordinary impact on your life. When we are used to attending to what everyone else needs, it is a radical change to regularly ask ourselves, 'What do I need right now?'

## It starts with YOU

I have often heard people saying that you need to know and love yourself before you can really know and love others, but I resented that because I felt as if I was a loving person anyway, but I just didn't know how to love myself.

What difference does a healthy relationship with yourself make for other relationships?

It means:

- People can get to know the real you, your true self, rather than the masked version you think they will like.
- The exposure of the real you creates opportunities for greater intimacy and connections.
- You will gravitate towards healthier relationships in which you are both equals.
- You won't build up guilt and resentment.

You can develop this relationship with yourself by working through the earlier chapters on getting to know yourself, feeling your feelings, and the exercise at the end of this chapter on getting to know your Inner Child and trying out new ways to show yourself love. As with any relationship, it requires time and energy — don't short-change yourself.

## Exercise 6 — Writing to/from your Inner Child

Find some time when you will be alone and undisturbed, and take your time. This is not a job that deserves to be rushed. Grab your journal and pen. Or you can download this exercise and all the exercises in this book from my website.

www.helensnape.com/dropthefakesmile

1. Address your writing to your Inner Child and introduce yourself. Tell them who you are — the healthy, adult version of them — and that you would like to get to know them. Feel free to ask them any questions you might have, such as 'What would you like me to know?' 'How are you feeling?' and 'What do you need?'

---

---

---

---

---

---

---

---

2. Pause. Breathe.

3. Now, you are going to tune into your Inner Child. If you are able to, write with your non-dominant hand when you write back as your Inner Child. Let it flow. Don't try to edit or analyse it as you go; just write. Keep going until there is nothing left, then pause and breathe. You might want to get up and move around a little.

_____

_____

_____

_____

_____

_____

_____

_____

_____

_____

4. Read back what your Inner Child has shared with you. If they didn't share anything, that's okay. They may take some time to do this. They may be pleased by your contact, or they may be angry. Know it's all okay.

5. You can now reply to your Inner Child and thank them for sharing with you. You can acknowledge the feelings or any information they have shared, and you can share with them what is true. Respond to what they need. Finally, let them know that you will be back with them again soon.

_____

_____

_____

_____

_____

_____

_____

_____

6. As you close this exercise, consider what you need right now. Maybe it's a walk, a meditation, a chat with a friend, or putting on some music.

# CHAPTER 7

# Asking for Help

I never wanted to ask for help. I should be able to manage my life by myself. If I asked for help, I was really admitting I was a failure. Eventually, though, I felt so desperate that I realised I needed professional help, but I was really the only one who could make that first move.

As I knocked on the therapist's door, I swallowed a huge feeling of shame. I felt like I really must have failed as a human being to need to seek out a therapist.

"Come in!" he called, and I entered a lovely, bright, cosy space with pastel-coloured armchairs and a thoughtfully set-out glass of water and a box of tissues. I was going to need those.

I didn't want to admit to the therapist, let alone myself, that I might need help. I had tried so hard in my marriage for so many years, and I didn't want to admit that it simply wasn't working. I also didn't want to admit that I, who considered myself an intelligent and educated woman, couldn't figure out where I had gone wrong or what the root problem was. I had achieved so much on my own; why wasn't it working this time? It was just more evidence there was something wrong with me.

I didn't really want to be seen as the mess that I was. I was used to hiding behind a mask where everything was fine, and I could get away with the fake smile.

I was very glad that I did seek help and go through with it, and I now see that the breaking down of my 'lone warrior' persona was the key to my letting all of the real me — my true self — come to the surface. I learnt that to continue this journey, I needed support, I deserved support, and it was okay to lean into that support.

## Why it is hard to ask for help

We carry around stories about why asking for help is bad, but we are not often aware of them. What might some of those stories be?

You might tell yourself that no one wants to help you, or you feel you don't deserve others' help, and that just isn't true. You have created a vicious cycle that reinforces this belief — you never ask for help, so no one helps you, and you begin to believe that no one would ever want to help you.

Or you believe that no one *can* help you. You are such a train wreck of a human being that you are beyond help. That is not true either, but I know it can feel like that.

You may see asking for help as being weak. You may pride yourself on being able to do things on your own, and you have achieved so much that you may feel shame for not being good enough to continue on your own.

You may find the prospect of being honest about your own human imperfections very hard to tolerate.

You may fear the vulnerability of opening up and asking for help. After all, if you ask for help, the answer might be yes or it might be no. You may worry about the other person's reaction to being asked. What if they are annoyed? What if they reject you? Could you handle it?

You may be protecting yourself from the possibility that if you asked for help, you might then be let down and be left with uncomfortable feelings of anger, which you would prefer to avoid.

It is also a fundamental hit on your identity. When you grow up feeling like no one can meet your needs, you may end up denying that you have needs and instead project them onto other people — *they* are the ones that need help, not you. It can challenge your very identity if you admit that you have needs, too, including needing help.

**What if asking for help made you *strong,* not weak?**

How might you begin to see asking for help in this way?

## What real responsibility is

What if, instead of having to do everything on your own, doing it right the first time and castigating yourself if you make a mistake, responsibility for your life looked a lot different?

Asking for help *is* taking responsibility for your life. No one can do everything by themselves, and no one is good at everything. It takes strength to recognise when you need help and to seek it out. After all, if the gas boiler in your house broke down, you wouldn't try to fix it yourself; you would call a gas engineer. We all need help sometimes.

You are not all-powerful, and you don't need to be either. You are not responsible for making the world run smoothly. A part of this journey is a spiritual one in which you discover your higher power and let go of trying to control everything (which you can't), and instead, hand it over to a power greater than you. This will give you so much freedom, and it is something we will come back to in Chapter 10.

Real responsibility also means no blame. When I say no blame, I mean both others and yourself. I knew that blaming others meant I wasn't taking responsibility for my life, and that was okay as I tended to blame myself for anything that went wrong anyway.

But what — I can't blame myself either?

How extraordinary!

Blaming yourself is punishing yourself, and it takes away your power. You can, instead, learn to recognise that you did the best you could at the time. You can own up to and learn from your mistakes and make any amends you need to. You can learn from your experiences and decide to do something different in the future.

You don't have to tell yourself off repeatedly and live with guilt and regret.

## What asking for help means for you

Your humanness, your need for help, means that you are like everyone else. You are not separate and different. You *are* enough.

This realisation might begin to open up a window of compassion for yourself and others in a new way.

When you ask for help, you are being honest with yourself about your needs and acknowledging what you are not so good at (or don't have the capacity for). You are recognising others' strengths, talents, and abilities, and in so doing, you are befriending reality rather than denying it.

When you get the support you need and that you deserve, you will grow faster.

Perhaps, most importantly, you will be prioritising your recovery. You will be prioritising YOU. This is a loving act towards yourself. You are taking care of your Inner Child. When you try to make progress on your own, it is so easy to slip back into old ways of thinking, feeling, and behaving. It takes so much effort to keep on track. By asking for help, you are stating to yourself and the universe that you are putting yourself and your recovery first. You are finding the support and perhaps the accountability you need.

### Where to find the help

You must find what works for you. You might find a therapist or a coach which whom you can work on your recovery. When you seek one out, check their credentials, have an initial meeting, and tune into how you feel with them. Do you feel safe and understood? Do you like their methodology or approach?

You might find a support group or recovery group helpful. It can be incredibly powerful to listen to the stories of other people who have had similar experiences, thoughts, and feelings as you. You will realise you are not alone and not as alien as you imagined. Sometimes, others' stories can help you remember experiences from your own life that help you put together the puzzle of how you got to be who you are today. When you feel ready, sharing your own story in a supportive group can be a wonderfully validating experience.

If you are lucky enough to have a supportive friend you know is a healthy adult with healthy relationships, you might want to ask them to tell you when you fall back into old patterns or check in with them whether your responses are healthy or not.

## Exercise 7 — Ask for help

For this exercise, give yourself 20 minutes and have your pen and paper ready. Remember, you can download this exercise and all the exercises in this book from my website.

www.helensnape.com/dropthefakesmile

1.  Use these prompts to write about your experience asking for and receiving help:

    •   How do I feel about asking for help?

    _____

    _____

    •   What do I make it mean about myself?

    _____

    _____

    •   How do I feel when I receive help?

    _____

    _____

2.  Make a list of any areas in your life where you are struggling or feel stuck. Examples could include health, wealth, career, intimate relationships, family, friends, and/or spirituality.

_____

_____

3. Pick one of these areas in which you feel stuck or are struggling.

   • Who might you ask for help with this?

   _____

   _____

   • What is the worst that could happen if you did?

   _____

   _____

   • What is the BEST that could happen?

   _____

   _____

4. Go and ask for help and see what happens.

# LOVING BOUNDARIES

CHAPTER 8

# Healthy Boundaries for Healthy Relationships

In my marriage, everything was my fault. If my husband forgot to take an important document to work, it was because I had burnt the breakfast muffins. If he spilt his lunch, it was because I hadn't made the 'right' kind of lunch. If he lost concentration when working from home, it was because I made a noise or was walking around too much. In that relationship, I didn't feel safe enough to speak up for myself or refuse to buy into his narrative.

When I left my marriage, I was determined to have different relationships, healthier relationships. I wanted to make sure I was showing up differently, and I was committed to doing the inner work to achieve that. Healthy relationships and emotional connections are the keys to our happiness. The brilliant news is that if we have experienced unhealthy relationships and maybe have some unhelpful relationship behaviours of our own (either from what we experienced growing up or from toxic or abusive relationships), we can un-learn it in favour of what actually works.

**Healthy, flexible boundaries turn out to be the key to safe, loving relationships.**

I am still doing the inner work. I believe it is a lifetime journey, and I can also already see what has changed. A friend asked me if I wanted to go to a particular museum she was keen to visit. I told her it was not my thing and suggested that we find something we would both love to do together. I wouldn't have done that a few years ago. I would have panicked, agreed to go, felt a sinking feeling, and tried to convince myself that I'd actually enjoy it. I would have gone because I didn't want to let my friend down — my emotional boundaries needed some work!

As I write this chapter, I realise that I could actually fill a whole book on boundaries, but we need to start somewhere and not try to change too much at once, so we don't get overwhelmed. Here are some top tips to get you started.

### Loving boundaries

I used to think that if I set a boundary in a relationship, it would push away the other person and create a rift between us, but with healthy adults, when you set a boundary, it actually creates safety and invites space for greater intimacy, too.

To give you an example, imagine Joanna and her partner, Lara. Joanna and Lara have been dating for a couple of months, and sometimes Joanna stays over at Lara's house with Lara and her children. Lara really enjoys these occasions and encourages Joanna to stay over more often. However, Joanna values time on her own in her own space. She needs that alone time to recharge.

What happens if Joanna doesn't say anything and goes along with Lara's wish to stay over more often? Well, Joanna wouldn't be honouring her own needs, and even if she didn't recognise them, it would generate feelings like anger, sadness, and fear. She may begin to resent Lara for wanting to spend so much time with her and she may begin to express her unhappiness in ineffective ways, such as being passive aggressive: slamming doors, sighing, and arguing about other things.

Lara will begin to notice something is off, but she won't know what it is, and she will wonder if she can trust Joanna. Joanna's dishonesty will have created a rupture in the relationship.

Instead, what if Joanna *did* set a boundary by taking the time she needed by herself? In doing so, she would be taking care of herself, validating that it is safe for her to speak up for her needs and wants in the relationship, which will honour her own agency and choice.

Lara can trust Joanna more because Joanna is being honest with her. Both of them will feel safe to raise any future issues, knowing they can work through them without drama.

Boundaries teach other people how you want to be treated. If you don't tell people, how will they know?

## Different types of boundaries

There are a variety of different boundaries. Below is a non-exhaustive list of areas in which we can all have boundaries. As you read through some examples below, note whether you feel like your boundaries in that area are too weak, too rigid, or fairly well-balanced.

### Time Boundaries

Melanie loves her job, and when she first started, she was careful to keep to her working hours 9-5. Then meetings went into her diary for 4.30/5.00 p.m., and she wouldn't leave the office until 6.00 p.m. Then she had so many meetings she had to check her work emails on the way home and again on the commute to work in the mornings.

Melanie was struggling with **time boundaries,** things like when you start and finish work each day, including checking work emails and phone calls, how often and how long you take rest breaks, which days of the week you work, and not working on holidays or sick days.

**How about you?**

Yes No
☐ ☐ Do you have boundaries about which days of the week you work?

Yes No
☐ ☐ Do you take the rest breaks you need?

Yes No
☐ ☐ Do you switch off work-related emails and calls when you are not at work?

Other examples of time boundaries:

Yes No
☐ ☐ Do you limit time with your family of origin (the family you grew up with) to what is comfortable for you?

Yes No
☐ ☐ Do you go to bed when you are tired and need sleep?

How are your boundaries in this area?

☐ Too weak?    ☐ Too rigid?    ☐ Well-balanced?

## Physical Boundaries

When Lisa separated from her husband, because she owned the house, she asked him to move out. He did move out, but he held onto a key. She came home from work one day to find him in the house. She was not comfortable with him having access to her home, so she asked him to return the key and asked that if he needed to see her in future, he call to make arrangements for when it would be mutually convenient. Lisa was protecting her **physical boundaries**.

### How about you?

Yes No
☐ ☐ Do you only let people into your personal space who you want and when you want to?

Yes No
☐ ☐ Do you protect your possessions and money, only lending when you want to?

Yes No
☐ ☐ Do you communicate which touches you like and which are unwanted?

How are your boundaries in this area?

☐ Too weak?    ☐ Too rigid?    ☐ Well-balanced?

## Sexual Boundaries

Tanya was devoted to her partner, and there were times she enjoyed sex. She noticed that what she liked and enjoyed varied depending on the time of the month. She also noticed that she most enjoyed sex when she felt emotionally connected with her partner. Her partner was more turned on by the physical intimacy and thinking about what they were going to do together. They each had their own unique preferences and limits, their **sexual boundaries**, and it took time for them to find out where they could find mutual pleasure and connection.

## How about you?

YES  No
☐    ☐    Do you know and communicate what you like and don't like and your preferences and limits?

YES  No
☐    ☐    Do you act with consent?

YES  No
☐    ☐    Do you discuss contraception?

YES  NO

☐  ☐  Do you exercise the right to change your mind at any point and allow your partner to do the same?

How are your boundaries in this area?

☐ Too weak?      ☐ Too rigid?      ☐ Well-balanced?

## Emotional Boundaries

When I lived with my ex-husband, I never socialised with colleagues after work. Why? Because he would manipulate my feelings, so I felt guilty for having a laugh with colleagues whilst he was at home working. I felt ashamed that I was selfish for enjoying something he didn't have. Then he would create a fuss about something seemingly unrelated later that evening as passive-aggressive payback for my going out. He didn't respect my **emotional boundaries,** and I didn't respect them either.

### How about you?

YES  NO

☐  ☐  Do you let yourself feel your own feelings without judgement?

Yes No
☐ ☐ Do you acknowledge and honour others' feelings?

Yes No
☐ ☐ Do you ask how others feel rather than assuming?

Yes No
☐ ☐ Do you refuse to answer inappropriate questions?

How are your boundaries in this area?

☐ Too weak?    ☐ Too rigid?    ☐ Well-balanced?

## Mental Boundaries

Pat was a successful and popular life coach. She had a thriving private practice, and other coaches respected her. Occasionally, she collaborated with other coaches on side projects. One day, she was contacted by a coach seeking a partner for a new project she was very excited about, except Pat wasn't interested.

Pat was worried that if she told the coach she didn't want to be involved, they would be really upset and might even be angry with her. Pat overstepped her own **mental boundaries** by assuming what the other person was thinking, though she had no evidence to support her assumption. In fact, the other coach was absolutely fine with Pat's declining her offer.

**How about you?**

Yes No
☐ ☐ How about your mental boundaries?

Yes No
☐ ☐ Do you hold your own opinions when others
don't agree?

Yes No
☐ ☐ Do you direct your own life rather than following what
someone else tells you?

Yes No
☐ ☐ Do you ask what someone thinks rather than
assume you know?

Yes No
☐ ☐ Do you allow disagreements to happen rather than
trying to smooth things over?

Yes No
☐ ☐ Do you ask before offering advice?

How are your boundaries in this area?

☐ Too weak?     ☐ Too rigid?     ☐ Well-balanced?

## Spiritual Boundaries

When I was growing up, I remember that my grandma always went to church on Sundays. If we wanted to see grandma for Sunday lunch that day, we had to go to church, too. It didn't matter whether we wanted to go or not; it was what was expected. So that is what happened. It was an overstepping of our **spiritual boundaries.**

### How about you?

YES   NO
☐    ☐    Do you trust your own spirituality and ethics?

YES   NO
☐    ☐    Do you follow what *you* think is right?

YES   NO
☐    ☐    Do you listen to your own instinct?

YES   NO
☐    ☐    Do you honour your own values?

How are your boundaries in this area?

☐ Too weak?    ☐ Too rigid?    ☐ Well-balanced?

What areas stand out for you?

☐ Time?    ☐ Physical?    ☐ Sexual?    ☐ Emotional?
☐ Mental?    ☐ Spiritual?

## Exercise 8 — Moving towards healthy boundaries

Get your journal out for an exploration of your boundaries. Remember, you can download this exercise as a worksheet and all the exercises in this book from my website.

www.helensnape.com/dropthefakesmile

For each of the type of boundaries listed above (Time, Physical, Sexual, Emotional, Mental, Spiritual), write down your answers to the questions given.

1. Do your boundaries tend to be too weak, or too rigid, or are they well-balanced?

 

 

2. What is one area in which you want better boundaries? What difference might this make in your life?

 

 

 

 

3. What is it that needs to change for you to create, communicate, and enforce this boundary in your life?

_____

_____

_____

_____

If you are new to boundaries, give yourself grace. It is like learning any new skill: we try, we make mistakes, and we try again.

# EFFECTIVE
# COMMUNICATION

CHAPTER 9

# Effective Communication

### Open and honest emotional communication

Being open and honest about your world and your emotions can seem terrifying if you haven't experienced this or seen it modelled. We wish or expect other people to be mind readers and magically know how we are feeling and what we need without us saying anything. We get resentful when they fail to do this even though it really isn't fair to them.

Your feelings are a part of your inner truth, and if you try to hide them or ignore them, other people can often tell, maybe not consciously, but they will know something is 'off', that there is a mismatch somewhere, that you are not being honest with them. On some level, they might recognise the fake smile for what it is: fake.

The place to start practising more open and emotionally honest communication is with people with whom you feel safe. This may be a therapist, coach, friend, or support group. As you begin to share how you really feel about things with safe people who won't judge you, you will begin to drop your guard and your fake smile and let people really get to know the real you. And the real you is worth knowing!

By choosing who you share with, you are also protecting your mental, emotional, and spiritual boundaries.

When you are honest with others, you are honest with yourself, too.

### Expressing your feelings

The most important thing you can do for yourself when it comes to feelings is to ask: 'How am I feeling?' and own the truth of what you feel.

How do we begin to be more honest with other people about what we feel when we are so used to pretending that everything is 'fine' and wearing that fake smile?

This is a vulnerable, tender, and courageous arena you are entering here, so you will want to choose wisely who you share your feelings with, especially in the beginning. We don't want to repeat old cycles of having our feelings invalidated or ignored by others.

Choose those people with whom you feel safe to begin opening up about your true feelings. Notice how you feel around different people and how they treat other people. You might find a friend, family member, coach, counsellor, or support group where you can open up without fear of judgement.

Something that I know bothers people in my community a lot and that I've found really hard is knowing how to express my feelings without offending anyone. One of the lessons of recovery I have learnt is that other people's feelings are not my responsibility.

Did you hear that?

*Other people's feelings are not your responsibility.*

That doesn't mean you have a free pass to be obnoxious, which is super unlikely anyway if you are a recovering people-pleaser! It means that whilst we can be mindful of what and how we say things and we take responsibility for what we say and do, we don't get to control or manage how other people might react or feel.

This is a part of establishing healthy emotional boundaries, allowing ourselves to have our feelings and other people to have theirs without taking responsibility for others' feelings.

## Nonviolent communication

One of the most helpful techniques I have come across for expressing feelings without blaming others or escalating a situation is to use nonviolent communication (NVC).[2]

The principles of NVC are:

### Observation

This is where you notice the facts. Instead of focusing on what you think about the situation, how you feel about it, or even what you guess the other person is thinking, focus on what your five senses are telling you: what you can see, hear, touch, smell, and taste.

### Feelings

This is where you slow down and ask yourself, 'How do I feel about this?'

Remember that there are no right or wrong answers. You don't need to justify how you feel. When you notice how you feel, you might ask yourself, 'Is there anything else I am feeling?' You then communicate how you feel, owning the feeling by using an 'I feel...' statement rather than a statement that blames the other person, such as 'You make me feel...'

---

2  Rosenberg, Marshall. (2003). *Nonviolent Communication: A Language of Life.* PuddleDancer Press.

Also, avoid making it into a story. If you find yourself saying something like, 'I feel like you don't respect me, and you can't be bothered anymore, and it makes me worry about where this relationship is going...' then you have gone into story mode, and your ego is in charge. It also makes it more confusing for the other person because how you feel gets lost in the story!

## Needs

This is where you identify and express your unmet needs. Connect what you observe with how you feel to figure out your unmet needs. It could be a connection, trust, understanding, and/or respect, to name a few.

## Requests

Once you have communicated your observations, feelings, and needs, you can follow up with what you want from them. Make it a positive request for what you want rather than saying what you *don't* want. We want to draw on their compassion and willingness rather than have them do something out of guilt, shame, or obligation.

Here is an example of how this might work in action.

Let's take the example of my partner, who normally does the dishes. He's now not done the dishes for a couple of nights, and I feel annoyed about that and worry that he isn't bothered about our relationship anymore.

The way not to express myself would be to show him a dirty plate and say, 'Huh! What is this? Maybe you can't be bothered to do this anymore?'

Instead, I can use the NVC technique, starting with Observation.

**Observation**
'You didn't do the dishes last night or the night before.'

Notice that this focuses on facts. It is what I saw happen. There is no assumption about why my partner has done this, and it also doesn't go way back into the past or make a generalisation like 'you *never* do this' or 'you *always* do that'.

**Feelings**
I could say something as simple as, 'When you don't do the dishes when you say you will, I feel annoyed, let down, and anxious about our relationship.'

Notice how this is an 'I' statement? It is about how *I feel*. It doesn't blame anyone, and it doesn't go into a story about why these events happened.

**Needs**
I could say something like, 'I need to be able to trust that you will do your share of the housework.'

## Request

Finally, I make my request: 'It would really help me if you could do the dishes before you come to bed.'


## Expressing wants and needs

When you have spent half of your life totally other-focused, it feels quite alien to express your feelings or speak up for your own wants and needs. Like anything else you want to learn, it takes practice, and it is going to feel awkward for a time. Don't let that deter you. Effectively communicating your wants and needs is your responsibility.

We can use the Nonviolent Communication (NVC) method again here. Let's look at the example of my being irritated with my partner for looking at his phone during dinner to see how I might communicate what I need.


## 1. Observation

We start off with a simple observation, focusing on the facts:

*When we have eaten dinner together this week, you have been looking at your phone during the meal.*

This is where you describe what you see, hear, touch, taste, and smell. Notice that there is no assumption about why my partner has done this, and it doesn't go way back into the past or make a generalisation like 'you never do this' or 'you always do that'.

## 2. Feelings

This could be something like 'When you look at your phone when we eat, I feel ignored and rejected.'

Notice how this is an 'I' statement. It is about how I feel. It doesn't blame anyone. Avoid making it about the other person, for example, 'You make me feel unwanted.'

## 3. Needs

This is where you express your unmet needs. For example, 'I need to feel connected with you when we eat together in the evening.'

## 4. Request

Once you have communicated your observations, feelings, and needs, you can follow up with what you want from them.

For example, 'I would really love it if you set aside your phone and talked with me during meals.'

## Conflict

Many people, including myself, who grew up not knowing how to set boundaries, hate confrontation. If you didn't see healthy conflict modelled while growing up, it is no wonder that you avoid conflict as an adult. If all you witnessed were people flying into rages, disagreements being swept under the carpet, or denials that arguments ever happened, it gives you no foundation or skills to handle conflict other than to hide from it!

Unfortunately, avoiding conflict is a lose-lose approach — you don't get what you want or need from the situation, nor do you support the relationship.

Conflict is inevitable in a healthy relationship, but it does not need to be a destructive force between you. Healthy conflict is a great way to clear the air. You do need to feel safe in the relationship first, though.

As you go on your journey of clarifying what you feel, what you want, and what you need (as opposed to what *everyone else* feels, wants, and needs!) and working on your boundaries, you will speak up for yourself more and more and not always agree with other people. That is okay. Our ego loves to know who is right and who is wrong. Our True Self sees beyond that.

## Exercise 9 — Healthy relationship behaviours checklist

1. Write each of the statements below in your journal, or download this exercise and all the exercises in this book from my website.

    www.helensnape.com/dropthefakesmile

**Healthy Relationship Behaviours:**

- I ASK what the other person thinks or feels. I don't assume that I know.
- I ask for what I need.
- I take accountability when I mess up. I apologise and make amends where I can.
- I change my behaviour when I recognise I've messed up.
- I listen to understand others' perspectives and not pick holes in them.
- I speak up for myself when someone hurts me.
- I share my feelings with trustworthy people.
- I spend time on my own.
- I accept the other person as they are with their flaws without trying to change them.
- I am willing to end a relationship that isn't good for me.

2. Pick one of the above statements that resonates with you.

_____

_____

3. Over the next week, find opportunities to try out this behaviour.

4. Journal about how you felt before, during, and afterwards.

_____

_____

_____

_____

_____

_____

_____

_____

_____

_____

_____

_____

_____

_____

_____

5. Write about any impact you notice it having in your relationships.

_____

_____

_____

_____

_____

_____

_____

_____

_____

_____

_____

_____

_____

_____

_____

_____

_____

# FUTURE YOU

# CHAPTER 10

# Letting Go of Control

I was in control of my life. I *had* to be in control of my life. The buck stopped with me. I remember reflecting on how uneven my marriage felt. There were periods when, aside from his work, my husband did nothing else except watch TV. Then there were times he wasn't working either. I had a full-time, demanding job in Human Resources, and I did all of the housework and cooking and taking care of all the bills. I even did the administration and taxes for my husband, and I did it all because I felt responsible for holding it all together.

**I felt I had to be the hope.**

It was too much for me to carry. Whilst I believed in God, I didn't feel any support in that way.

When I left my marriage and began my recovery journey, I joined a recovery programme that included a spiritual element. I baulked at it, unsure I believed in God anymore, and even if I did, I didn't want anything to do with a God that had let me go through 18 years in such a disastrous marriage. Then I attended a talk that gave me an entirely new perspective on the whole 'God' thing.

The speaker explained how many of us carry around a concept of God that comes from our childhood experiences of authority figures. In my case, that meant an intimidating, strict, loud, unempathetic male.

Yes, those were definitely included in my concept of God.

They went on to explain that it doesn't have to be that way. What would you like your Higher Power to be like instead? I desperately wanted my Higher Power to always be there for me, listen to me, guide me, and love me.

That was when I *knew* that She was there and always had been.

And suddenly, I didn't have to be the hope any more.

*You* don't have to be the hope any more.

## What's this spiritual stuff got to do with control?

My experience, which echoes many other people's experiences, is that I had to hit my rock bottom before I was willing to ask for help and prioritise my recovery. My life had got out of control, and that is often where you start your recovery journey, when you can't take it anymore, and you have to admit your life has become unmanageable.

Out of that chaos, you want to get back into control of your life, and understandably so. This can take many different forms, from changing eating habits to getting enough sleep, from building a support network to trying new hobbies, and from tackling your debts to learning how to be more mindful of your thoughts and feelings.

You gradually get clearer on what you need and want in your life, and you make space for it. This is all a part of the recovery journey.

And then you have to let go.

I know, I know — it seems crazy. You have to go to all of this effort to get your life into some sort of order again.

I don't know why it works like that, but it does. When you can truly let go of something, it is much more likely to come back to you, or something even better will come along.

133

This is where the spiritual element comes in — how can you let go of something if you are the one in control of your life and you have to be the biggest authority? You can't.

If your concept of a Higher Power is one that is judgmental and vengeful, you won't want to give up control to them either.

What you *can* do is let the Higher Power of *your choosing* take over running your life. You can give your burdens to them. You can entrust them with your needs and wants. It doesn't mean that you stop taking action; you continue playing your part, but this time it is without the world on your shoulders.

This journey of going from chaos to control to letting go of control mirrors the development of your spiritual relationship, whatever that may look like for you.

### What you can control

Control is such a big theme in recovery. We often don't like our realities, and we give too much to the relationship and don't get back what we need. We don't like it, and we want the other person to change. We see their potential and the potential for our relationship, and we help them in an effort to get *them* to change.

I didn't think I was controlling. Hahaha. I just really wanted my husband to be happy, so I tried being as nice and as giving as

I possibly could be, ignoring my own needs and feelings so he could be that happy person, but it wasn't my job to change him. I didn't have that power.

You don't have the power to change other people. Now, you might protest if your beloved has changed their behaviour because of your pleading or persuasion — beware! When someone changes under pressure from someone else, it breeds resentment, and the change is often short-lived.

What can you control, then? You can control everything within your locus of control:

When we focus on what we *can* control, we own that over which we have power, and we establish and protect our boundaries.

## You have a purpose

You have a unique purpose in this world, and it isn't to please other people. You are a spirit in a human body, and you are here for a reason. As you develop your relationship with your Higher Power, you will begin to perceive what that purpose is. It might be to be a great mum, to contribute to your community in some way, to share your story on the stage, or to hone and use a skill or talent with which you have been gifted.

You may not always see how life's events are leading you in the direction of your life's purpose — the path is never a straight one — but you can check in with your Higher Power when you have decisions to make, whether it takes you closer or further away from your life's purpose.

Checking in with your Higher Power can be as simple as asking for help and being willing, open, and receptive to the response. Your asking could be a prayer; know that you don't need to get the words right — your Higher Power will know what is in your heart. You may receive a response straight away, perhaps an inner knowing, or it may take time. Or the response might be to 'wait'.

I like to journal about the issue I am grappling with or the decision I need to make, and as I do that, I offer it up to my Higher Power for guidance. I then meditate to listen for a reply.

## Spiritual boundaries

Your relationship with your Higher Power is sacred, and no one gets to mess with it. If someone tries to tell you that God doesn't approve of something you are doing, you don't need to listen to them because you have direct access to your Higher Power, and you can ask them yourself!

We each have our own unique spiritual experience and spiritual relationship. Growing up, you may have been told that God is a certain way and has certain expectations of you and how you can communicate with God. You don't need to be bound by what others say. Your spiritual relationship is just that: yours.

If this is all new to you, you might want to try exploring different spiritual practices to see what you are drawn to. Some examples include being in nature, meditation, visiting a holy place, or writing.

## Spiritual practices

There are many spiritual principles and practices that support doing the inner work on this journey of recovery. Acceptance, non-judgement, trust, and forgiveness are just a few. One practice I have seen make a big difference in my clients' lives, and my own is the practice of gratitude.

A gratitude practice is really helpful because it helps balance out your brain's natural negativity bias. Through evolution, our brains have been hard-wired to seek out what's wrong to help us survive and keep safe. Our brains still try to do that, even though we no longer live with the constant threat of being attacked by a lion! A gratitude practice helps us notice the positive, and therefore, get a more rounded and whole picture of life.

You don't need to find 'big' things to be grateful for (although those are great, too). It can be noticing those things we often take for granted, for example, a beautiful sunset or cloud formation, the smell of the grass after it has rained, the softness of a t-shirt, the hard work that our limbs do for us, or the kindness that someone has shown us.

You can create your own daily gratitude practice by writing down three things each day for which you are grateful, but don't leave it there — we don't want this to become another tick-box exercise. Once you have written down what you are grateful for, read through your list slowly, letting each one really land with you, and notice how you feel.

## Exercise 10 — Your Higher Power

If you struggle with the concept of a Higher Power, this exercise will help you. Remember, you can download this exercise and all the exercises in this book from my website.

www.helensnape.com/dropthefakesmile

1. Think of some authority figures who were in your life as a child.

2. Write down how you would describe each of them.

3. Now, write down your current concept of God. What are they like? How do they treat people, especially you? How do you feel about them?

_____

_____

_____

_____

_____

_____

_____

4. Notice the similarities and differences between your current concept of God and the authority figures from your childhood — how have those authority figures shaped your concept of God?

_____

_____

_____

_____

_____

5. Now, write down how you want your Higher Power to be. You are no longer constrained by your existing concept or what anyone else says. Let your imagination create a Higher Power you would love to have in your life. Write freely.

_____

_____

_____

_____

_____

_____

_____

_____

_____

_____

6. Consider one thing you can do to explore your spiritual relationship further.

_____

_____

# CHAPTER 11

# Dreams and Goals

I'm not sure I used to have dreams for my life, not real ones for my True Self, anyway. I studied psychology at university because I wanted to understand myself better and other people, too. I was busy projecting my own needs onto other people, and I'm sure that's what led me into a helping profession. I also had a feeling that I 'should' strive to enter a profession where I could advance and make good money so I could lead a comfortable life and show that I had not 'wasted' the university education my parents had paid for.

What was truly in my heart at the time, I'll never know. It was too covered up with the drive to understand my own insecurities and the expectations of family and the wider society.

In my personal life, you could say I had dreams, except now I would describe them as fantasies. I had the Hollywood fantasy of meeting a man who would love me as much as I loved him, and I would then feel whole. Instead, I met a judgmental and vain man, who, after charming his way into my heart and my life, had me starving for the scraps of affection he gave me. I knew he had a troubled childhood, and I held onto the fantasy that if I loved him enough and supported him enough, he would become the man I longed for. Fantasy.

Nowadays, my dreams come from me, my True Self and my Higher Power. I dwell on those dreams to let them take shape. I create goals that are stepping stones to my dreams and then plan how to reach those goals.

### It's okay to dream

When you have lived for so long, putting your focus on others, it can feel wrong to dream about your own life, but if you don't do it, who will?

What has stopped you from dreaming about your own life? Perhaps you have never considered it because your parents guided you or told you what to do with your life; it's never too late to start dreaming for yourself.

How do you feel about dreaming about your life? Maybe it will bring up regret that you didn't do this sooner. Be kind to your past self about this. You are a different person today than you were even yesterday.

Maybe you feel it is wrong to dream. Maybe you feel it is pointless to dream. Maybe you feel some excitement that, at last, you *can* dream about your own life.

**Give yourself permission to dream.**

Your dreams matter. You matter. Letting yourself dream is another way of loving yourself.

**Where do you start?**
What can help you start to dream for your own life?

Give yourself a quiet space and time to dwell on your dreams. Make this a regular practice. You don't have to start big. If you have no idea what you want for your life in ten years' time, that's absolutely fine. How do you feel about imagining what your life will be like in a year? Six months? Next week? Find the level you are comfortable starting with.

If even that seems too much for you, start with what you *don't* want.

## Exercise 11 — The don't want/do want lists

For this exercise, take a blank piece of paper and draw a line down the middle. You can also download this exercise and all the exercises in this book from my website.

www.helensnape.com/dropthefakesmile

1.  In the left column, put the title 'What I don't want', and in the right column, put the title 'What I do want'.

2.  Now, consider what you *don't* want in your life. Maybe you don't want drama in your life, a mean boss, too little sleep, or never seeing friends. Write down everything you can think of in the left column.


**What I don't want**                   **What I do want**

_____              _____

_____              _____

_____              _____

_____              _____

_____              _____

_____              _____

_____              _____

3. Then, for each item in your 'don't want' list, in the right column, write down what the *opposite* of that would be for you. For example, if what you *didn't* want was 'family members staying at your house when they visited', you might write that you want to 'enjoy time with family when they visit during the daytime and have my house to myself at night'.

| What I don't want | What I do want |
| --- | --- |
| | |
| | |
| | |
| | |
| | |
| | |
| | |
| | |

Pretty soon, you will have a list of things you *do* want in your own life. As you get to know yourself more, your dreams will take a firmer shape.

### Goals bring dreams into reality

It's very exciting when you begin to dream, but If you don't do anything else, those heartfelt longings may remain unrealised. You need goals to help bring those dreams into reality.

Goals are like the different towns you might pass through on your way to your final destination. You know when you have reached them because they are well-defined, and when you reach a goal, you can celebrate!

Let's say your dream is to live in Paris. What needs to happen or change for that to be possible? Maybe you will need to research about living in the city. Maybe you will need a visa. Maybe you will need to learn some French. Maybe you will need to save some money. Maybe you will need to release some fears about moving to another country. You might speak with people who already live in Paris or who have moved to France to find out what steps they went through.

You can begin to make a list of every step you will need to take and in which order. You can then assess which steps are vital and which are 'nice to haves', and you can create super-clear definitions of each goal, so you know when you are there.

For example, instead of 'I will need to save some money', it might become 'I have saved £2,000 for relocation expenses.' Ideally, you want your goals to be SMART goals. These are goals that are:

Specific
Measurable
Achievable
Relevant
Timebound


Goals are incredibly helpful in creating order out of what can be woolly ideas. They show you the direction you need to head in and how far you have to go.

You can keep your goals under review, too. As your situation changes, you acquire new information, or if the unexpected happens, you can revisit your goals to check that they still make sense for you.

If you want help converting your dreams into goals, this is where a great life coach comes in to help you get that clarity, define your goals, and give you support and accountability as you work towards achieving them.

You deserve to live a life you love, so give yourself the gift of working towards your dreams, one goal at a time.

If it feels scary, this idea of creating and working towards goals, give yourself some compassion. Any change in your llfe, any uncertainty, even if you know it's leading towards a better life, is going to challenge your ego's desire to stay the same, to stay safe and small. Remember, it's YOU, your true self, that is choosing the way.

## Exercise 12 — Looking back

As we draw near the end of our journey together, here is one final exercise to help you start to dream. Remember, you can download this exercise and all the exercises in this book from my website. www.helensnape.com/dropthefakesmile

It's an exercise of the imagination by travelling into the future. Set aside 30 minutes when you have quiet time alone to let your imagination run free. You might like to go on a walk for this one.

After you have completed the exercise, you might want to journal about what came up for you.

Imagine you are 90 years old. You are happy with your life. You are sitting in your favourite, comfiest chair and reflecting back on a life well-lived. From this serene space, you consider these questions:

- What has been my proudest achievement?
- Whose company have I most enjoyed?
- Where have I loved to visit or live?
- When did I feel most free?
- What was my most important life lesson?
- What is my lasting legacy for this world?
- If I could give my younger self (you today) one piece of advice, what would that be?
- What is it that I want my younger self (you today) to know about themselves that they don't already know?

# CONCLUSION

Congratulations! You have made it to the end of our journey together. We have covered a lot in this book, and you have been on your own journey throughout. What has really jumped out for you? What is one thing you will do differently, stop doing, or start doing as a result of reading this book?

I hope that one thing we will *all* do is drop the fake smile. May you never have to smile to keep the peace, take care of someone's feelings, ignore your own feelings, or fit in with someone's expectations of you. May your smile always be genuine, easy, freely given, and often used.

Feel free to go back to re-read this book whenever you wish or dip into chapters that call out to you. Trust that you are learning what you need to learn at that moment.

Know that this journey you are on, recovering from people-pleasing patterns, is the journey of a lifetime. It won't always be plain sailing. Some days you will feel frustrated by other people or yourself. You may see yourself going backwards or getting diverted from the path you want to follow. That is to be expected. This recovery from the disease to please is not a linear journey. Falling back into our old patterns from time to time is a part of the process and may show up new things that we need to learn or how to put into practice something we have already learnt. Be kind to yourself on those occasions. Be kind to yourself anyway.

Someone much wiser than me described life as a spiral. We keep encountering the lessons we need to learn in this lifetime in new ways as we make another circuit of the spiral.

Keep coming back to yourself. You have been looking to other people to give you the answers that only you can know for too long.

What links all of these chapters together are five key areas to develop your genuine smile:

**S**elf-Discovery
**M**ind-Body Connection
**I**nner Child
**L**oving Boundaries and
**E**ffective Communication

These are the five pillars that I work with my clients on every day and I see how this inner work blossoms into their external life in better health, better jobs, better relationships and enjoyment of life.

As you move forward from here, know that you are changing, even when it doesn't feel like it. When you plant a seed, it doesn't usually produce a plant or even a shoot overnight. You give it the light and nutrients it needs to grow, trust that it *is* growing, and practise patience. One day, the shoot will appear!

You are whole. You are enough. Your True Self will guide you as you break free of old people-pleasing patterns and move on to a life of peace and power.

*"I am not what happened to me, I am what I choose to become."*
– **Carl Jung**

# ABOUT THE AUTHOR

Helen Snape is an award-winning relationship coach who helps women develop balanced and rewarding relationships at work and at home by building boundaries, self-confidence and effective communication skills.

A recovering people-pleaser herself, Helen knows first-hand what it is like to experience burnout, due to constantly over-working. She also knows what it's like to lose self-worth in a long unhealthy marriage.

Helen has been coaching for over 10 years, has a degree in Psychology from the University of Warwick and is qualified in mindfulness, body-oriented coaching and coaching with trauma. An award-winning speaker, Helen has been interviewed on BBC Radio, the Women's Economic Forum and been featured in Happiful magazine. Helen is also author of *Building Healthy Boundaries — an over-giver's guide on when to say Yes and how to say No in Relationships.*

Helen lives in Surrey in the UK and as an empath, her greatest joys are spending time in nature for replenishment and in water for support and general delight.

# HELEN'S SERVICES

You can access Helen's online self-study course 'Better Boundaries for Better Relationships' to help you move towards relationships at work and home where you feel respected, where you know and are able to communicate your boundaries and be able to handle pushback and others reactions effectively, here:

🌐 https://www.helensnape.com/betterboundaries

Helen's vision is to grow a community of women consciously creating healthy relationships for themselves and for future generations to come.

Learn about Helen's other services, including one-to-one coaching, here:

🌐 https://www.helensnape.com

You can also connect with Helen on social media:

f https://www.facebook.com/HelenSnapeCoaching

📷 https://www.instagram.com/helen.snape

in https://www.linkedin.com/in/helensnape

🐦 https://twitter.com/HelenSnape3

# RESOURCES AND FURTHER READING

## Book Resources
www.helensnape.com/dropthefakesmile

## Helensnape.com
Helen Snape offers numerous resources for recovering people-pleasers on her website. These include:

- People-Pleaser Blog
- 'Better Boundaries for Better Relationships' online self-study course
- Workshops
- 1:1 and group coaching

## Further Reading

Beattie, Melody, *Codependent No More; How to Stop Controlling Others And Start Caring For Yourself*, 1986, Hazelden

Powell, John, *Why Am I Afraid to Tell You Who I Am?*, 1969, Argus Communications

Chalfant, Michelle, *The Adult Chair; A Guide to Loving Yourself*, 2017, Michelle Chalfant

Glover, Robert A., *Dr., No More Mr Nice Guy; A Proven Plan for Getting What You Want in Love, Sex and Life*, 2000, Running Press

Peck, Scott, M., *The Road Less Travelled*, 1978, Arrow Books

Jeffers, Susan, Ph.D., *Feel the Fear And Do It Anyway*, 1987, Fawcett Columbine

## Conscious Dreams
PUBLISHING

Transforming diverse writers
into successful published authors

www.consciousdreamspublishing.com

authors@consciousdreamspublishing.com

*Let's connect*

Printed in Great Britain
by Amazon

49911229R00090